Welcome to the world,
little one!

We hope you learn
to love Machine Learning
as much as we do.

Love,
Your AdTheorent Family

To all the little machines roaming around my house,
thank you for helping me to get work done.

Visit us on the Web!
www.tinkertoddlers.com

Contact us!
tinkertoddlerbooks@gmail.com

Tinker Toddlers supports early STEM learning. STEM is an acronym for science, technology, engineering, and mathematics. We provide simple explanations about emerging STEM concepts to the littlest learners to help facilitate the absorption of complex details later in life.

Introducing STEM early has shown to improve aptitude in math, reading, writing and exploratory learning in a wide spectrum of topics.

Machine Learning!

for KiDS

Dr. Dhoot

Tinker Toddlers®

airplane

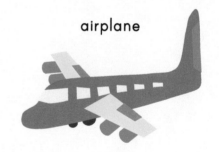

crane

truck

dump truck

police
car

Do you see **machines**?

windmill

Chugga-Chugga CHOO-CHOO!

train

car

Machines are outside.

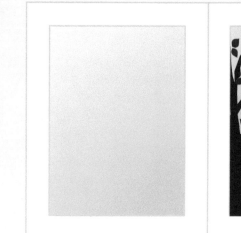

smart speaker

laundry
machine

Machines are inside.

vacuum

vroom!

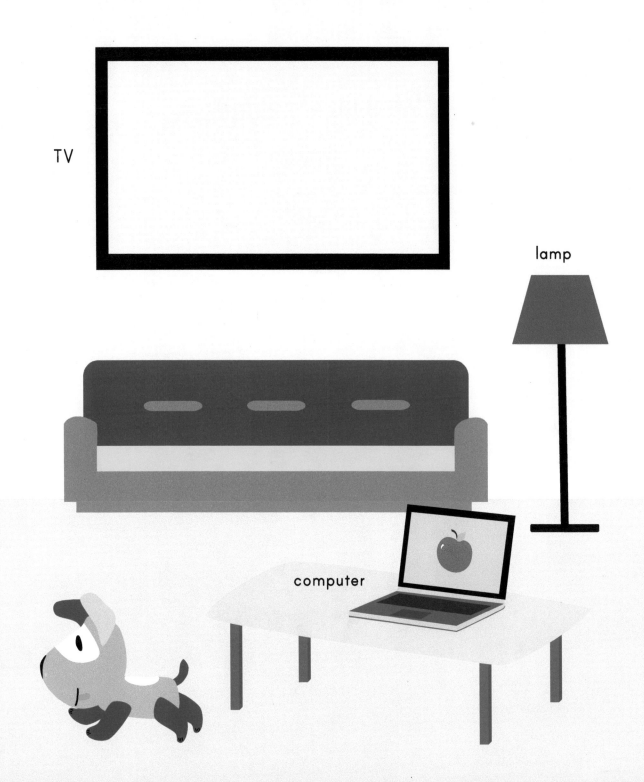

TV

lamp

computer

Machines do work.

laundry machine

Computers are machines.

computer

Just like you,

computers can draw.

```
**Draw Apple**
> Turn on
> Draw apple
> Color red
```

They do what you tell them.

Instructing what machines should do is called **programming.**

Just like you,

computers are getting smarter!

How do we get smarter?

More data
helps us learn and build!

We gather data, process and make decisions.

Computers do this, too.

Machine learning programs, called **algorithms**,
perform better as they get more data.

You can learn.

You have **human intelligence**.

Computers learn, too.

They have **artificial intelligence**.

We are taught what's
right and wrong.

This is **supervised learning**.

We learn on our own.

This is **unsupervised learning**.

We also learn by getting rewarded.

This is **reinforcement learning**.

We learn from experiences.
Learning together gives
more time to play!

Glossary

Artificial Intelligence: the power of a machine to mimic intelligent human behavior.

Computer: an electronic machine that can store and work with large amounts of information. This info is called data.

Human Intelligence: the ability to learn, understand things, or deal with new or difficult situations.

Machine: a piece of equipment that does work when it is given power from electricity, gasoline, etc.

Programming: developing and carrying out various sets of instructions to enable a computer to do certain tasks.

Reinforcement Learning: reward-based learning that helps a machine to learn how to act in a certain situation.

Supervised Machine Learning: learning where data is clearly labelled and the output is given. Used for solving classification and regression problems.

Unsupervised Machine Learning: learning where the evaluation is qualitative or indirect. Used for solving pattern-based or structural problems.

Questions for your budding learner

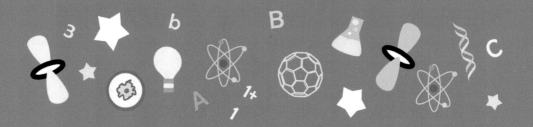

Machines help us to get work done.
What would you want to teach a machine?

Machines are everywhere.
What machines do you have at home? Which one is your favorite?

The robot in this book is a machine. Its name is Robo.
If you had a robot, what would you name it?
What would it look like?
Draw it out on the last page and share the picture by posting a review!

My Robot_____

To share, go to order history at place of purchase, locate product, and click on "Write a product review"!

Dear Reader,

I hope that you enjoyed reading about machine learning!

Science and technology are evolving rapidly and it can be hard to keep up. I hope you and your little learner(s) enjoyed learning the very basics and continue to build your knowledge base.

If you liked this story and want to read more like it, there is a whole series of Tinker Toddlers books on Amazon, just waiting for you.

Best,

Dr. Dhoot

www.TinkerToddlers.com
tinkertoddlerbooks@gmail.com

Tinker Toddlers' Growing Library

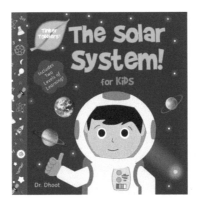

amazon.com/author/drdhoot

tinkertoddlerbooks@gmail.com

Industry experts, scientists, engineers,
parents, and kids contribute much of their time to ensure
Tinker Toddlers is successful at supporting early STEM learning.

To support our efforts, please:

1) go to order history at place of purchase
2) locate product
3) click on "write a product review"
4) tell us what your favorite part was

CPSIA information can be obtained
at www.ICGtesting.com
Printed in the USA
BVHW021959080621
609034BV00005B/16